TAKEN UP!

I love You both
and Thank you so much
Jan Stuck
7/12/14

Unleashing the Holy Spirit
Spiritual Journeys Toward
a Bigger Picture

Taken Up!

Joan Stuck

To order additional copies of this book, contact:
Xlibris Corporation
1-888-795-4274
www.Xlibris.com
Orders@Xlibris.com
114369

CONTENTS

I delayed the inevitable, and if I had it do again, I wouldn't take so long. Unless that is his plan!

ACKNOWLEDGMENTS

Being able to share such a small part of my journey toward spiritual growth has been a privilege. Walking with Christ while writing this book has blessed me on so many levels of appreciation and with a deeper understanding of what our benefits are in having him in our lives daily. I thank God for my relationships with my children, who will always be an important part of me and have taught and given me a reason to always look forward. I also thank my extended families and the mentorships I have grown with and again have found boundless encouragement in as well. They always accept me for who I am and who I have become and who I will be, always planting the seeds that I can by sharing my stories and the truth in God's word. And to Christ Jesus, who has always been here and helped guide me to understand his purpose of how I may serve. Amen.

Chapter One

I would lie for hours in my grandfather's strawberry fields while I'd stare up into the clouds and dream of something bigger, a place to be, all the while making pictures in the clouds of cotton. Was there anything larger for me to be part of?

I knew dirt farming and how to grow anything placed in dirt. I enjoyed my grandfather's company so much even though I wasn't nurtured sitting on his lap; he would make me and my siblings feel a part of his life as though it was ours too. One of my first groundbreaking experiences was when I was eight years old and he said, "You can get on that tractor and pull it around for me up over by the barn now, and I'll be along shortly." I had only watched and observed and listened while sitting with him on the tractor, but I knew I was ready; this was the confirmation that he believed in me. It was a promotion into young adulthood to be trusted with this enormous task that was expected at least by the age of ten, so I figured I was doing well.

We all enjoyed him during the harvest seasons as he would walk up and down the lined rows and talk to the workers or sing songs out loud and encourage them. I was young, and I am happy the memories I have of him are joyous and good. My grandfather died when I was a young teen.

Although I worked on my grandfather's produce farm, there was no future in it for me as only men in the family inherited the land. It was the way many of our foreparents believed as women would marry into their future. However, in this world, things were changing—the Vietnam War was still going on, women were merging into the workplace more, and divorce was on the rise in historical numbers. I was fourteen and one of eight children; seven of us were girls.

By the time I was almost sixteen, my family was not exempted from the effects of this new world; my parents also joined the ranks and divorced. Their private affairs were kept pretty secretively from their children; however, being from a small-town community, it seemed our neighbors knew more of their indiscreetness than we did. I and my siblings knew they had problems, I just didn't believe they would divorce ever.

I grew more anxious as a teenager growing closer toward adulthood and with no plans for a real, grounded future. I had great and grand ideas of what I'd like to do; however, the monies weren't there. I moved in with my mom at seventeen and began work.

At eighteen, I was able to obtain a grant, and this gave me choices to work on a couple of construction crews for a minimum wage. I picked the road crew that was building bike paths in the nearby larger city. I was hoping for a larger scale of opportunity like going into physical therapy or studying writing. I was told to take this grant until perhaps a better one with a larger opportunity showed up. I worked hard and was happy for what I learned in an area I never would've picked or planned to learn.

I also had seen that there may have not been a future for me to make something of myself in if this was all that I could get.

As it showed later in my life and in many trials and errors in my life's choices, God proved to me that he had always been here. He had a plan. It was a presumed knowledge to most that I was saved, but to the world, I was peculiar and unidentifiable.

I knew there was something bigger than me. Someone or something put this all together.

Have you ever stood at the crossroad of your life and thought deeply of who you are in this universe and gathered the reality shots that you are just a speck when detected through the lens of a high-powered microscope? And then and only then it hits: nothing will change unless you get up and go.

A light goes off! And you are at the crossroad of life, and you make that decision. The decision that has no guarantees, but at least you will be moving.

When you finally come to the realization, it's because there has to be more. Perhaps a key that turned this all on . . . or off.

You see it in other people's lives that appear to be happy, successful, and fulfilled. When things are great, wonderful, hard, or unfair, there has to be a key that you put in place, and when turned, it changes the outcome of the circumstance—life!

Oh, I may have been considered naive by some. Mostly, though, I found others who agreed and were searching just as much as I was.

I was not alone.

I believe we were born destined! Oh yes, I do!

According to Corinthians 2:7, "But we speak God's wisdom in a mystery, [even] the [wisdom] that hath been hidden, which God foreordained before the worlds unto our glory."

I learned that God did know us before this world!

I discovered that God knew us before the worlds foreordained us unto our glory.

And if that weren't strong enough, he revealed this to us by his Spirit!

According to Corinthians 2:10, "But unto us God revealed [them] through the Spirit: for the Spirit searcheth all things, yea, the deep things of God."

So what happened?

We were destined !

Planned!

Developed!

Deliberately, by a God who wanted us.

With me being raised in a church, you would've thought I heard that. But I didn't.

Many of my friends were searching for the key the same ways I did.

Instead of hearing this from the pulpit, we would discuss it at times among ourselves.

"Yes to all parents out there."

They do discuss life to one another out here! I know, for instance, a conversation I have reflected on a few times. I remember something as this (a little role-play):

Myself: What do you think about there being a God out there?

Cyndi: I'm not sure, but I overheard my mom and friend talking, and they see physics that tell them they've been here before this life.

Me: Really! Were they important?

Cyndi: I don't know, but because they didn't learn anything, they're here again.

Me: Really? Then what did they say?

Cyndi: They laughed and held up their drinks, cheered that it'll be interesting how they can mess up this one.

And with others I shared with, I would learn we were different creatures on earth previously and we moved up the chain for good behavior to now being a human.

After that one, I wondered.

Evolution has bounced from fish to apes.

The thing is, we all have this spirit God gave us long before we were born.

Whether it is living, growing, or being suppressed, it is here in us!

What I mean by a suppressed spirit is when we don't acknowledge the spirit in us.

The spirit God gave is *not* suppressed by any means.

Even before God created the heavens and earth, we were destined. I really don't hear too many people who actually deny if Jesus was real!

I hear just about anything else except this. We know he lived here, was born here, breathed here, was a teacher, claimed healing, and showed us how to prosper.

God loved, shared hope, taught of peace, and taught faith. And yet it's hard to wonder what the problem is.

Why doesn't everyone hop on the hope wagon and ride?

The answer is because God is a God of free choice. He doesn't twist our arms or break our legs to fall down and worship him. Love doesn't work like this.

We have so many misconceptions about God not being any of these things. Mostly I have found that most do not seek ye first the Kingdom of God.

I knew there was a God; I just didn't know who God was . . . yet.

I even defended him only because I thought that was what you were supposed to do. Until that day came when I asked, is there a God? Or is there something else, perhaps magic, maybe spiraling spaceships that watch our every move, deciding who should join them next? I just didn't know.

CHAPTER TWO

One particular time in my life was hard for me. I woke up one day with two kids, and after going through a divorce and spending the last seven months partying and building strong ties with my new forever-partying familyhood, I seemed very bold, and clearly, I could not stay like this.

I felt the urges and knocks that this would probably have to cease sometime, and so when it did became clear, I couldn't stay in this mode either. I gave heed to the nudge I had been feeling. It wasn't a condemning nudge. It was a get-up-and-*move* nudge. I could hear a voice saying, "Have better plans."

This was before I ever knew a relationship with God!

So vividly he (God) nudged me, and I heard the voice tell me, "This is not my plan."

So as what any nonsaved child loved by God would do, I took action; I quit partying again and began planning my departure from that which was familiar toward a path less traveled.

I sold mostly everything I had, and what I didn't sell, I abandoned it.

Off I went to find the key. I suppose I was looking for hope!

Sometimes life has a way of awakening you when you get so caught up in what it is you think you're doing that by time you finally figure it out, you're already neck-deep in a sandpit and you don't realize that there is no way but *up* to get out.

So about two months later and eight hundred miles away farther and almost out of cash (by the way, no cell phones back then), I looked for and found the closest emergency welfare office.

It was already closed for the day as I remember, and it was I and my two children in a 1967 Datsun wagon. In an unfamiliar place, I took up parking in the lot of the welfare building and figured I would stay there overnight. I got the kids out of the car to stretch and play a little before loading them both back in the car, and as we were calming down to rest, an officer drove up and informed me I couldn't stay there. So I drove around trying not to forget my way back and found a very busy grocery store.

I thought, *Good, busy, lots of people. I should be able to get some sleep here.*

I was more concerned of my two children who were now sleeping.

They were small, and I nested them with the two blankets I had, and totally oblivious to our crisis, they fell asleep. About an hour passed when a man came knocking at my window and asked if I could help him. And as naive as one could get, I figured that by stepping out of the car and a few feet away from it, I was protecting my children from harm's way. However, the stranger asked me for money; I told him I didn't have any. He proceeded to raise his arm above my head, and as his arm was flying down to hit me, I reached in an instant and grabbed on to that stranger's arm; and somehow, without knowing how to this day or remember, he ended up bent over with his head between his legs on the ground, mumbling, "Okay okay, I give!" This man was taller, larger, and stronger. I immediately jumped back in the car and drove off.

Oh, God works in mysterious ways.

My two children woke up and asked what was going on, and at that very moment, I heard it again.

The voice!

"Go back to the parking lot you started in." My first thought was I may get arrested, and so I reasoned in my mind about the officer, then again the officer may have been done patrolling for the night.

After I arrived back to the welfare parking lot, again my children were already sleeping and I talked to God directly. I said, "God, Jesus, Father, Son—I'm not even sure what to call you. I could use a real friend right now!

"If you are real, please show yourself to me, and I will believe the rest of the days of my life. I must know that it is you, or this won't work between us. Please show me, Lord, if you are real."

It wasn't fifteen minutes later before I heard another knock on my car door, and this time it was a woman. She said to me, "They will come back, you can't stay here. I live across the street with my kids, and I have food and cocoa for your kids and a bath. Please come."

My instincts felt good about this lady, yet my instincts were already tested. She spoke again; this time she said, "Please, my name is Adeline, and it would mean so much if you would come. I have a Bible, and I would like to share with you." My inner heart thoughts were slow to react—*ticktock, ticktock.*

A lot of thoughts stirred through my mind, and then I looked into her eyes and saw a beautiful blue-eyed Hispanic woman with a sincere heart to get my family off the street for the night.

I drove the car across the street and parked in front of her home. My children were awakened one more time. Adeline made us toast and the kids cocoa. She helped me clean them up and then lay them down for the night. She asked where I was from and what was I doing there. As I explained, she listened. She shared with me how to ask for assistance the next day. And then she pulled out the Bible and read from it. I was so tired and yet I do remember a couple of mentions,—*Jesus, loved, world, forever, amen.* I perked up for a moment and told her I asked for God to show himself to me if he was real. And Adeline smiled calmly; she said, "Let's ask him together," and we did. I remember the part, "I believe in the name of Jesus, Amen."

I went to the welfare line first thing in the morning and was there all day. The lady who worked my case said to come back the next day. I told her I needed to feed my kids! She told me even the shelters were full, and I needed to come back the next day.

I don't know why I had so much pride. I probably could've gone right back to Adeline's for another night, but I couldn't bring myself to that place to ask. And I didn't have to. Thank goodness she was waiting for me by my car and asked if we would come on over one more night in her home. And we did. This time I asked questions. Her husband was not living there, and she was raising her children alone. We shared and I learned she was really having some hard times as well. And yet she afforded my family's food, shelter, and the word!

What was so dumbfounding to me was at this moment, I realized her eyes were not blue as I remembered; they were now hazel. I asked her if she ever had blue eyes, and she paused for a moment and shook her head and kind of looked at me strangely and then shrugged her shoulders, smiled, and said, "No, only what you see, hazel."

Now I have to ask, do you see where God was through this?

Absolutely, he was there, right up and personal. He was in my face! And yet I wouldn't acknowledge him. Because I didn't know him . . . yet!

The next day, Adeline waited for my children and me to come out from my appointment; I received a very small amount of help. I remember Adeline saying not to worry about something and, the birds in the air, I looked up and figured it had to mean something biblical.

She asked if we'd like to spend the day and one more night as I was planning on another road trip out of this area the next day. So she took me to parks where I saw painted bridges, and we went by a zoo and drove through a very intimidating neighborhood and then to her home, safe and sound one more night.

She prayed over us and for us and prayed for angels around us or another, and I accepted it as it seemed good. I needed prayer; I was out here with two kids, and this could get a little scary. The next morning, she gave me her phone number and address and asked that I get in touch with her again one day. I gladly took it and promised that one day I would pick up the phone and call her.

CHAPTER THREE

MOVING ON

I was looking for the freeway when I realized I was still wearing my wedding ring on my left hand now. I don't know why I didn't notice this before, and right in the corner of my eye, I saw a pawnshop. I needed the buildup of *any* monies, so I stopped in; and also while up, I took a gold cross and necklace out and pawned them.

At the sweet, tender young ages of only two and three, my children asked, why did I give that man my jewelry? And I told them both, "Because I love you so much.

"And mommy needs the money to help us out."

What a blessing even in hard times children can be.

Well, I headed back toward the overpasses to get to the freeway; and at three o'clock in the afternoon, we were on our way. Slowly ever so slowly yet we were on our way through the rush hour traffic.

About an hour into heading east and almost clear of the moving parking lot I had been in, I came across a hitchhiker; he was dressed in leather-strapped sandals and a fitting white robe garment. He stood maybe six feet with dark curly semilong hair that touched just the back of his garment.

I know what you're thinking.

Why am I picking up a hitchhiker! Right?

Well, I pulled over as traffic was barely moving and picked him up. He said his name was Tony. Are you still asking why am I picking up this hitchhiker?

My answer is because a voice inside me said, "He is safe. Pick him up," so I did.

Tony was safe; he did most of the talking, like, "Where are you from? Where are you heading?" I kept my answers short. I appreciated his company, and I didn't even think about the robe and sandals he was wearing anymore. Tony was heading more toward Colorado in looking up a friend. He was nice and polite. He asked where was I going, and I told him Arizona; he asked why. And I told him I had a friend there and I hoped to work and live there. His presence was peaceful, and he was helpful as well. He picked up the radio off the floorboard in front and toyed around with it until it worked; we had a lovely eight——to nine-hour drive before pulling in to town at approximately twelve midnight. He asked me if I knew the address of where my friend lived, and the truth was, I did not. I had planned to call her the next day,

It was at this moment he opened the glove box, and he pulled out a letter I had received from her about four months prior, which had her return address on it. For only a moment, I thought with wonderment how that letter got in there! He then helped me find this address for the next day by physically driving to it.

Tony was like an angel. We then found a hotel not far from where she lived with two beds, one for him and the other for me and my two children.

We slept uninterrupted till 9:00 a.m., which really refreshed us all. The next morning, he thanked me for the ride as we left the room, and I thanked him for his company as we parted ways with the words *good luck* and *be safe*.

Hindsight is always clearer than foresight. As I reflect back on these times, I must ask, why I was so obviously being protected time after time I put myself at harms way with two children!

Looking back, I would never recommend a single woman and her children to go out into the world like this. However, when the Lord nudges you, and, you know there's a key to be found . . .

I listened to the voices and acted on them.

By now I have long realized I have taken dramatic approaches to finding change and growth for my life. However, the spirit of God was with me! I learned years later that I had family and friends who prayed for me during these times. More so, I believe someone had the spirit of faith and believed I would be watched over and kept safe during and through these trialed times. My grandmother told me years later that she had prayed for me. She didn't know what she needed to pray for yet believed. I know that in Romans 8:26-28, it says, "Likewise the Spirit also helpeth our infirmities: for we know not what we should pray as we ought but the Spirit itself maketh intercession for us with groanings which cannot be uttered. And we that searcheth the hearts knoweth what is the mind of the Spirit, because he maketh intercession for the saints according to the will of God.

"And we know that in all things God works for the good of those who love him, who have been called to his purpose."

Then I remembered what the Lord said in Acts 11:16-17: "John baptized you in water, but you will be baptized with the Holy Spirit."

So if God gave them the same gift as he gave us, who believed in the Lord Jesus Christ, who was I to think that I could oppose God?

You see, without me knowing God in a relationship and someone who loved the Lord praying for me, I was protected as I weaved in and out of one trial to another, searching for, well, a key. By now I must say I'm not so sure it's the key I needed to find. To a single mom, anything would work at this point to provide some sort of safe stability.

So I went off to look up my friend.

I first found a pay phone and called her, letting her know I was in town. She invited me over happily. After talking, I made plans to stay with her family until I found work and a place for myself and children to live. It wasn't easy.

Again I went to the welfare office and applied for what I could. I also went to every business I had seen to apply for a job. My friend helped me so kindly up to the third week, and then I was asked to leave. The situation was uncomfortable, and injustices of circumstances were assumed without facts. And really I agreed that I didn't belong there in her home any longer.

Although she never spoke to me one on what it was that bothered her about me being there, I have forgiven her for that circumstance long ago. While I was out job hunting, she had found a lead on an apartment that was rent-free for the first three monthes with a year's lease. So she didn't toss me or my children out on the street. For this I have thanked her. I went and checked it out and took it. It didn't matter to me what type of apartment it would've been; in all truth, I was excited to take it.

And again I thank her for this, and as it later turned out, this was part of God's plan.

A couple of years later, that friend looked me up because she now needed a favor; I felt excited and fortunate as I was able to oblige her.

The day I took that apartment, I had found a job washing dishes at a family restaurant on ten-hour shifts.

This was a huge milestone—from zero to minimum wage. I had to begin somewhere. I met two women who turned out to be friends at this restaurant. The first one was Ross, and she was close to my age with two kids quite a bit older than mine. See, she had married at fifteen and began having children young and divorced young as well. We shared something in common at the job. She was a waitress whom I witnessed getting sexually harassed, and I too had been harassed by the same man.

We didn't complain because we both knew how hard it was to get a job. The owners allowed me to bring my kids to work most of the time, and I was able to keep them close-by and watch them as I would single-handedly wash the dishes and keep up with them even during the one-night-a-week all-you-could-eat fish fry. It felt like I slaved for them.

Ross met a new man while there, and the two of them made quick plans, and she moved with her two kids to Colorado.

And then there was Carol, who took Ross's job; she was the harvester of God's divine plan in my life.

Carol had made a couple of gestures to know me, and not to be rude at all, but I just was too busy with life to notice. One evening as we were both leaving the restaurant, I felt the urge that I would really enjoy a drink the old-fashioned way—in a bar. I would've never gone by myself, so I probably never would've gone if it hadn't been for Carol extending an invitation to go with her and her husband. We really hit it off well. And it was so nice after months of not knowing but only one other person to share with and she moved. To just be able share and learn about others was thrilling. Carol was a fireball for the Lord. She reminded me a lot of Adeline. She seemed pretty bent on driving the message across. I didn't mind at all because she showed the incredible love and kindness of the Lord in her eyes and toward others; she was just purely happy!

The following day she asked me to visit her church, the Church on the Rock. And I did. I really like it. Afterward, she asked if I'd like a Bible, so we went and got one. She didn't have a lot of money, and neither did I. Literally every penny I made was needed, but those nine dollars were well spent.

At this time during my life, with all the transitioning that had taken place, I was experiencing a lot of heavy, hard responsibilities that were not coming together for me. I desired so much better for my kids, and night after night, I would find myself crying alone after laying them down for the night. My visions were to be able to spend time with them more than I had, playing with them, picking out new toys with them, and being able to read a book to them and buy a new outfit for them and eventually moving to a better neighborhood.

All these things and events were now clearly not going to happen with my schooling or job experience. It seemed hopeless for me that I would be able to excel. I tried going to a trade school and had to quit short of graduation because I became ill, my car died, and I had child-care issues.

I had to make a choice to work where there was money coming in. Although it wasn't enough, it was more than no money.

The depression had sunk in without my awareness. I was hopelessly a mess. I tried with all good intent to keep a nice face, yet I would catch a glimpse of my reflection in a window and see how I was deteriorating in my emotional health. It was written all over my body.

Sometimes you may see such a person in passing, and now I had learned what low self-esteem looked like.

I really loathed being at another person's mercy. It is hard to borrow for me. This is why to this day I pay my debts, and if I help another person, I do not hold it over their heads as if it were a blackmail arrangement. Give with a joyful heart or loan with a joyful heart.

My children and I spent the evenings visiting Carol. My children were able to play in her apartment and enjoyed it.

My children, by the way, were great! They sensed how hard I worked. They sensed my struggles and loved me. I loved them too.

Carol had really driven home the scriptures over weeks of studying. One evening, a friend of hers from upstairs came down, and I was shooting questions and firing away like never before. They were both hungry to find the answers and debate them.

Chapter Four

COVERED

As the evening passed by, I grew tired and said my good nights. As I was walking to the door with my children, I felt the feeling of abandonment.

I felt that if I walked through that door, I would be alone.

I turned toward Carol and I asked what this was. Her reply was, "I know that feeling. It is because you're in a covered territory."

As I reached for the door and began to turn the knob, she asked me, "Are you all right?" And I answered, "Yeah, I think I am." She offered me then to stay longer or even spend the night. But in my mind, I wouldn't have it; that would've been a pity call. She replied, "Okay then, I'll see ya later." I replied, "Okay."

As I walked the children home, every step seemed heavier and sadder. I didn't want my children to see me feeling like this.

I wanted to cry and knew I was having a hard life, but really, I hadn't begged from anyone.

The kids would eat before I would. I was not going to be a burden. I had felt heaviness, and I began having thoughts I had had before but now was unable to suppress them like before. I got the kids cleaned and into bed, even said a prayer, and kissed them each, letting them know I love them. As now it was late, I found myself feeling horrible, worthless, and like a complete failure. As I sat alone in the living room, I wasn't even able to squeeze a lighthearted thought! Only masquerading negative thoughts played over in my mind. *Look what you've done. You are worthless. Those kids shouldn't be with you. Why are you here? No one cares about you.*

I was experiencing a suicidal takeover in my mind. After a while of pondering thoughts of ending it, I found myself sitting on the couch, asking God, "Why? I asked if you are real to make yourself known! Am I undesirable even to a *God*! Who is this God?" I had a pen and paper next to me, and I needed to write something on it for the sake of my kids and found myself looking down at my arms, scoping where to best begin the incision and end it. My mind was moving pretty rapidly.

Just as I was approaching that moment to just do it, I heard a knock at the door. I heard it and had no intentions of opening it; my door was locked, so I sat quietly waiting for whomever to leave. Again, *knock, knock*. Again I sat quietly, waiting for this person to leave.

Next, the door opened ever so slowly, allowing the light from the outside corridor in. My eyes were dilating as I tried to make out who just open my locked door with only a turn of the knob. All I saw was a small feminine figure shadowed from the light behind her.

She would ask, "Hey . . . Are you all right?" A few seconds must have gone by before she asked again, "I said, are you all right? Where are the kids?"

Then I answered, "They're in their bed, asleep." By now I saw this was Carol, and so she replied, "I think it would be best we get a few things and bring you all over to my place *at least for the night.*" Carol had clearly accentuated the latter part to make it clear that *we* were coming with her!

I remember silently thinking to myself "why would I go with her," and as she walked toward me and stood in front of me with her piercing eyes, she simply confessed, "I knew there was something familiar I felt before you left earlier. I wasn't able to figure it out, but then I finally did. You cannot be alone right now, so hurry up. Let's pack up the kids and go."

And amazingly, now I was on board.

What just happened? A divine intervention?

I was missing every opportunity God was throwing at me for at least a year now. As I'm sharing with you, I know you must see them! And yet this is what God does!

My pride blinded me, my immaturity kept me from wisdom, and impatience stole from me.

This and yet God still allowed me to feel his nudges and protected me from *myself*!

If you fall from an airplane without a parachute, the law of gravity says you will eventually hit bottom. And no matter how often I would escape one hit, I'd find another way to jump and not hit. After a while, you get tired and start asking yourself, "Is there really a bottom?"

I had a friend whose addiction to drugs led her to ask herself the same questions. Nance was a beautiful young mother of the most beautiful two sons one could hope for, and her addiction ate and ate into her family till all that she had was gone. At that point, I had no way of reaching her and handed her to God for his willing love to manage. It's easy to see what others' needs are at times, and yet this is why the relationship with the spirit of God is so crucial. God communicates with the same Spirit (himself, God) as he raised Jesus from the grave with. It's having that relationship inside of us that allows us to hear, feel, know, and communicate with *him*!

According to Romans 8:11, "But if the Spirit of him that raised up Jesus from the dead dwell in you, he that raised up Christ from the dead shall also quicken your mortal bodies by his Spirit that dwelleth in you."

There it is again!

Corinthians 2:12 says, "Now we have received, not the spirit of the world, but the Spirit which is of God; that we might know the things that are freely given to us of God."

The thing is, If God is for us, who can be against us? Certainly not the Spirit that has been given freely to us.

We are all sinners, and God made this pretty simple for our basic understanding.

We receive and believe! And he releases.

According to John 3:16, "For God so loved the world that he gave his one and only Son that whosoever believes in him shall not perish but have everlasting life."

You know, I have had more people tell me that the reason they don't step foot in a church is because there are too many perfect people in them. I have heard this more than any other comment about the church. And my response to that is they need to go back and ask why they are there. It is because God sent Jesus here for the sinners, not the perfect people without sin. Again, we are reminded in

John 8:7 that "if any one of you is without sin let him be the first to throw a stone at her."

It was late, and so I picked up my children as Carol assisted me back over to her place across the street. We settled the kids back down to sleep for the night. And she put on a pot of coffee and began firing the questions away. This was going to be a down and personal night. I had not yet shared with her a lot of deep-layered personal information about myself. And so now the questions began. "How long have you been down here?" I replied, "Not long, about nine months."

"How long have you been single?"

I replied, "Twenty months."

"And have you had any help? Are you seeing anyone now?" And probably a minimum of twenty other questions. She shared related instances, and I could appreciate that. I did have a question for her though. I asked, "How have you known God? How do you know the ever-loving Trinity? The Father? Who is Jesus? What is the Spirit? Who is in charge?"

She asked me, "Are you born again?"

I sat there for a moment and stared at her and in space for a moment. I had to think about this.

I replied, "I was born!"

_____

She said, "Wait right here. I'm gonna go get the neighbor. He will help me explain this."

And then she left for a couple of moments.

Now there I was, sitting at the table, enjoying a hot cup of coffee at approximately nine at night. And I was thinking to myself, "This is exactly what I did not want."

Being surrounded by religion solicitors was not my idea of finding the true God. I have to tell you though, I knew by now I was close to finding the truth. If I could just find out who he was, all my problems would be solved; I could then go straight to the source and finally ask the man in charge!

They came walking in together with his Revised King James Version *and* the concordance!

I had learned about God, the Father and the Creator; Jesus, the Son of the living God; and the Holy Spirit, who is God-given to Jesus, who ascended onto him at the moment of death and returned through the living spirit of God!

And who can live in us!

They would ask a question, and I would ask a question. And so I asked the biggest question of all:

How much would this cost?

They took a couple of seconds out, looked at each other with stretched-out smiles across their faces, and then answered, "Jesus already paid the price!"

"Huh. I hate to sound ridiculous. You mean I fall short my whole life, I am a torn, wretched, unclean, guilty sinner with a horrible past, and in the end the Lord is willing to touch me and clean the past from me and I can start anew?" I said all this as tears were flowing and streaming for the first time in months.

As I choked and gasped for their patience, I fought through the barrier, determined to get where it was I was going, which was trying to keep me shut up and locked out!

I finally began to see more clearly. I knew this was the key—*scratch!* The answer! All I had to do was say, "Yes, I do!"

It was then that they paused and Carol asked, "Do you want to get born again? And receive Jesus Christ as your Lord and Savior?"

And I replied, "Yes, I do!"

She then replied, "Let's pray and give your life to him. Repeat after me.

"Lord, I am a sinner. Please forgive me for all my sins. Please come into my heart. Forgive me of my sins. Be my Lord and my Savior in Jesus's name. I believe I have been forgiven of my sins. I believe, Lord, you live in me, and you are my Lord and my Savior. In the name of Jesus Christ, a*men!*"

I was born again!

And during that prayer, I closed my eyes and I saw a high priest wearing a white robe with a yellow turbine lining. I felt the love of God, ever so serene and warm, literally flow through my veins.

What is there to say about all this? I had made so many choices with undesired consequences,

and he was not done!

Carol looked at me and then continued to ask with joy in her eyes, "I now recognize and confirm with no doubt that you are born again! This, by the way, is the same as getting saved. "

So she proceeded to ask, "Do you want to be filled with the Holy Spirit and speak with tongues as the spirit gives utterance?" And within another twenty minutes and maybe ten scriptures later, I closed my eyes and received the gifts of the Holy Spirit! It was supernatural. I began using my new prayer language immediately, and I was embalmed with the Holy Ghost and anointed by all his grace.

I felt lifted as I basked in the love of the Lord.

I was speaking a new language now, which brought on to me the Holy Ghost giggles!

I knew with zero doubt at this moment, as I received Christ into my heart for the very first time in my life, that my body experienced being filled with the Spirit of the Almighty God!

And as I can explain best, Jesus Christ brought me clearly into my new life with a definite vision; I was filled with the warm Spirit of love I had never experienced and no man has ever been able to compare to.

I began my new relationship with a real being, and the scriptures now took on a new meaning for me. The Holy Spirit, now being so real, guided my understanding.

The word *infinity* is still not enough to describe the endless *mercy* and *grace Jesus* surrendered himself for. One does not know the truth without first developing a relationship with him. Only until then can one actually bare a fair, knowledgeable opinion.

CHAPTER FIVE

NEW

The first year of my new life, I practically ate the pages of the Bible as I hungered for all knowledge found in the pages of this book.

I was able to see and understand as I never had before. You see, I was seeing the hidden messages God professed in his word and that were now living and breathing in me.

I was amazed by the fact that God conquered so many wars and led others to prosperity and still others to destinies of their own. And yet none of it would have been possible them without listening to him.

I would like to share though that this is why having a relationship with the Father, the Son, and the Holy Ghost is imperative.

I developed a keen sense to protect my loving Father. As any relative who is close to the family would be, I now would be offended when someone in public would curse using the name of my Father. I was now one of those! I was a born-again, Bible-thumping, Spirit-filled Christian and almost always knew a scripture to rebut any nonbeliever out here. I was a baby Christian, which was the term for it in the great "80s.

I did mature more in my relationship with Christ, and he has always stayed true to me. He has worked on me lovingly and with patience, molding me and guiding me.

When I look back, I see a clear trail of where he was with me when before I had doubted. I really was a hard rock to crack; I was capable of finding the troubled road to destruction all by myself. I hold myself accountable for misguided choices I made as I was rebellious. And yet he was there waiting, just waiting, *for me*!

As soon as I confessed I believed, the angels sang and welcomed me into the kingdom of God's eternity.

Christ has never once condemned me of sin, not ever!

I see condemnation in the world. Many of us do this unknowingly when we talk about others or share an opinion. Some of us condemn others, believing this will change them. It doesn't work. Shame and condemnation only handicap the one spreading it and the one receiving it. No matter how carefully or precisely you choose your words, guilt or shame does not heal or change.

When the love of Christ began living in me, it evicted the old spirit living inside me, and *the loving conviction of God* took desires away from me I have never missed. I became a new being.

I once met a young man years ago after being saved. He tried to sway me and plant seeds of doubt that would've worked when I was still searching, except now I knew different.

I had Christ living inside of me; his very Spirit resided in my being, and so I already knew what he was saying was not true.

To an unbeliever, though, this would've definitely watered or planted seeds of doubt.

His opinion was serious; as he shared, he said, "Think about it, a man who can walk into the wall of your body cavity and take up living space? And then instantly give you the learned behavior of good and evil? It's a scam! These so-called churches where people call themselves believers and saved have raised millions of dollars to take care of themselves? When there are all these other people out here starving on the streets? Really, it's a worldwide cult—this Jesus Christ thing. They just want to get you in there and mind control you so you're already conditioned for one massive takeover."

Whoa!

I was praying on how to engage with an answer that would serve the Lord's purpose, not mine. Anything less would have not accomplished his will.

I could feel the love of God's nudge on this as it was his will for me to answer only as I could. You see, God knows my personality and how I come across to people, and he picked me this day at this moment to witness a man of clear doubt. As I finished talking silently to God about this, I answer to God, "Well okay, Father, I will answer him, but you know only because you said to."

So I responded to the man of doubt and looked him in the eye with gentleness, and as soon as I opened my mouth, the light of God shone through me. I answered, "I'm happy to share with you what I know is true and thank you for allowing me to share the love of Christ as I know him. He does take residence inside me because I asked and gave him permission. And with every fiber of my body, I can account that he is real."

Now for some, that may not have been the answer to share with such a doubter. On this day, though, that is what Christ had me share. And when I was finished with this simple answer, this man looked at me and replied softly, "Then would you please share with me and show me where I can find this man Christ and meet him, so I can have the same light and love that you have with him?"

I did share, and I also led him to a church where he could learn more, and he did get saved. I have seen him once since then, years later, up on a stage in a choir of another church I once visited. That's when I realized I didn't know this man's name. I was so happy and had wondered where he ended up. I never doubted though the seeds Christ had planted in this man.

In life, we grow up and we learn.

Some become educated to find a job, some begin their own business, and others seek alternative ways to live. Some may decide what some consider a home is not for them; others dream and find ways to obtain as big a home as they can imagine.

Some entertain themselves with programs to stay positive and find ways to keep positive energies surrounding them so they can feel the security to obtain the dreams.

And although some of these programs are good—yes, I said *good* referring to some of the programs—it is impossible to know or grasp the idea of truth! Our Father in heaven has a will so much bigger, so much more than you can imagine, and that's the freedom he wants with you.

He wants your dreams, ambitions, and goals.

For you to take it to him and share the desires of your heart.

Ask him for the way to obtain. Give our Father permission to live out your desires.

He can protect you from the doubters and cover you with the conquering Spirit of Christ.

There is nothing you can search the world over and find that would show he doesn't already have the creative knowledge of already knowing where to find and how to obtain.

If you have the faith the size of a mustard seed, you can say to this mountain, "Move," and it will move. Some of our mountains are smaller; some are larger than others. Yet if it is your desire, then you can ask it.

As I shared earlier in my testimony, I asked who you are. Where are you? Please show me. And he was always there like the time I was parked at the grocery store and a stranger tried to attack me or when Adeline came up to my car and asked my family, the three of us, into her home. He was there. He was there waiting, only I was blinded by my pride and allowed it to take me.

Freedom. There is no better freedom than in the love of our Lord Jesus Christ. Although he suffered unimaginable pain, he has allowed us a choice. The choice to receive him into our hearts and confess him as our Lord and Savior. Or freedom to choose another idol and worship that. It's true. Now a lot of Christians may not finish this book because of that statement. But it is the truth.

I'm not preaching a religion. I'm sharing a relationship!

There is only one way *to know* Jesus as the Lord and only one way to *receive him* as the Lord and Savior, and there are many other dictators who claim they are God—no different than in the old days of Egypt—of today in the world! There are many religions that loudly proclaim they are the ones. And many clubs that say the key of freedom is in their great books of knowledge. And then there are those who say "I don't follow any of them." They will claim, "I am not a believer of anything. I just exist." And yet that is a belief all in itself.

What I'm saying is, no one can truthfully form a truthful thought or opinion of who Jesus is, if one has not actually known Jesus? Nor can anyone not form any truth or make claims of who he is not until this person has actually known him.

And yet I speak so boldly, and he has given us so freely his devoted love, sacrifice, salvation! The Cross!

Chapter Six

COMFORTER

Years ago, I was carrying my sixth child, and I lost her before my sixth month of pregnancy. I cannot explain the loss of a child you love, carry, and plan for and prepare for and who is then taken instantly without notice. I wept and actually thought back to all the past sins in my life as to why would God allow this to happen. I remembered many reasons why God may have taken my baby.

I was filthy, corroded with past sin, and that was why he took my child. And then I was nudged and I heard him say boldly, "No! None of those reasons are true." That night after I put my kids to bed, I retreated to curling up on an old lounge chair, and then he reminded me that my sins were forgiven and buried at the cross the moment I received him as Lord and Savior of my life. I reflected back at the hospital and began to weep tears as I lay in there in a bed, and they brought my baby to me and then the Lord showed me how she was a blessing not only in my life, but in others' as well. Even though she never lived outside of my womb, she was a heavenly, God-blessed soul who made an impact on lives before she left to go home to be with the Lord in the heavenly realm.

Weeks later, after I had gone home from the hospital, the Lord gave me a dream.

I saw my baby, and I was able to hold her as he handed her to me. I held her up and looked her in the eyes, and she knew me. I saw the joy in her. And as I held her, I heard the voice of the Lord tell me she is safe. And I spent as much time with her as I needed, and then the Lord received her back, and I was completely at peace. How many physicians and psychologists will tell you that a dream like this is made up in the self-conscious mind to ease the pain of the victim? And I will tell you this is a relationship with the Holy Spirit!

We can see in Genesis 31:10-13 that "you can read where an Angel of the Lord came to Jacob in a dream and told him he needed to leave the land."

God can give anyone he chooses a dream; as we have seen, Pharaoh was given a dream, which Joseph was asked to interpret in chapter 41 of Genesis.

It says in Kings 3:5 that "at Gibeon the Lord appeared to Solomon during the night in a dream and GOD said "ask for whatever you want me to give you.'"

Acts 2:17-18 says the following:

> In the last days, God says I will pour out my Spirit on all the people.

> Your sons and Daughters will prophesy, your young men will see visions, your old men will dream, Even on my servants, both men and women,

> I will pour out my Spirit in those days and they will prophesy.

What I'm sharing is all throughout the word of God. Our Lord has made it known that we are walking around with his Spirit in us, and he can relate to us as he chooses and as we allow by having a relationship with him. We honor by choosing him, yes, and we will have better understanding.

Imagine just meeting for the first time someone that you had heard only rumors about. Now up to this point, you only have reserved information and an opinion based on information you have obtained.

Now you have actually met this person, and you disagree or maybe agree and can add to the information you were given because you now have an informed view of this person. As time goes on, you may develop a better relationship as well, and now you are a better judge of how this person's perceptive views are.

I'm just saying.

Although sometimes life, as we call it, happens, our Jesus is our comforter in times of need. I am not alone.

I choose and I wanted and I searched for Jesus and found he is the truth and the way. When I look in the mirror, I am not a person who lies to me about how I look. I am an older woman. I show signs of getting older and aging, and yet when my Father looks at me, he sees a child.

There is no need to dissect my words and see if there are any hidden meanings, or obvious meanings for that matter, as to why I made the choice to choose Jesus, because there is nothing irrelative to the question itself. We can search and layer reason upon reason to this oldest question on earth. Nothing has ever been refuted as much or has stood in time. No other topic has been kept alive, talked about, searched, discerned, or agreed on as the love of Jesus Christ has.

In many of my cries for help, I used to beg the Lord and often bargained with him for my needs, and then I read that Jesus will supply me with all my needs. And not only that, his angels will sing praises when I take my petitions to him.

You see, by going to Jesus, I show I believe! I have faith; I trust in the Almighty!

There was a large span in my life when my kids were young and I watched every penny spent.

It was difficult even with me being a master of couponing, buying farm produce and secondhand clothing, and watching the electric bill and the gas for transportation. I am sure many of you can relate.

Recreations were creatively free, and by time it came back around to me, but there wasn't enough. I went without needs that I've seen most women take for granted. It wasn't until one particular year that it was so hard: I had lost an income, we had a death in the family, medical expenses from the kids being sick were mounting, and the budget wasn't getting any larger.

I was sitting in the kitchen, staring out the window, when a bluebird landed on the edge of the bushes that lined the front wall of my home. I took notice because birds didn't come up this close to the home, especially when the window was open; I had kids in and out the door all day long.

Hmmm, that was nice, I thought to myself. The next day, a dozen or more finches came and visited my front lawn. Now I had lived there for five years at that point, and that just didn't occur even if finches were so common, not in my yard. Okay, so these are normal, possible coincidences maybe.

Or maybe not! These occurrences were happening after prayer.

Now some people may not appreciate doves as I do, and yes, over the course of the next week, I was visited by doves! And a couple of red birds, and again after praying.

This was now alerting my senses because two of these wild birds actually flew in the front door, paused on my counter, and without panic, flew back out. And then if things couldn't get more peculiar, a very expensive privately owned cockatiel flew into my home shortly before my children got home from school. Once they got home, we then put up signs all over our area: "Found bird. Please call." And within forty-five minutes, we received a call. Shortly after, a lady showed and offered me reward money for this bird. I refused the reward because I was trying to show my children to do unto others as you would want done unto you.

As this lady was leaving, she slipped a check on top of the tall speaker box in the living room and told the kids not to tell until she was gone. And they listened well.

As she was leaving the driveway, they rushed to show me the check she had left! It was enough to pay the remaining rent I needed. Oh, what a blessing she was. And I sang praises that night.

The next day, as I was walking out to check the mail, a dove landed on top of the mailbox and actually perched on top and watched me reach in and grab the mail. I closed the box, and if you can get a vision of what I experienced here, the dove then escorted me to my front door by flying low past me then perching itself again at the foot of the front entrance where a clay pot sat. I laughed inwardly with praise as it was a joyful play-by-play gift from the Lord to have fun like this with his creatures.

I remembered having the Holy Ghost giggles.

I put the mail on the table and began contending with my daily chores.

Later, after I took a break, as I was shuffling through the endless envelopes of bills and past due statements, a strange envelope had caught my eye.

It didn't have a return address, and I looked at the postmark. It was smudged, so I couldn't tell what state it traveled from. It looked and felt like possibly a greeting card, and it was addressed to me.

I didn't have any special occasions near, so without more to guess, I opened it, and out poured dollar bills of different denominations, enough to pay every bill I had for the remainder of the month.

I don't believe the birds magically made money appear. However, I do know, and I praised God more joyfully because the birds reminded me not to worry.

Jesus shares with us the following in Matthew 2:25-26:

> Therefore I tell you do not worry about your life what you will eat or drink or about your body what you will wear. Is not life more important than food and the body more important than clothes?

> Look at the birds of the air they do not sow or reap or store away in barns, and yet your heavenly father feeds them. Are you not more important than they?

And so I believe God has a sense of humor.

This experience began a domino effect of faith walks for me.

You've perhaps heard the saying, "When the student is ready, the teacher appears."

My faith began growing stronger by the day, and I grew more assured in my relationship with the Father as I grew.

God is so good! As I began to live free from bondage, I was given a gift to find amazing beauty in people of all walks.

I also found myself so amazed by the strength of the women in my life. There are amazingly strong women in my life. In my family and extended family and my close friends, I find single moms raising boys to become men. Married women working to carry the load after their husband lost their income. Moms and aunts and grandmas, sisters, and friends believing by faith the promises of Christ.

Some are working two jobs. Others are being creative and sell crafts and quilts, recipes, and some learned services. Others iron or prepare taxes, and the list goes on and beyond.

And I watch them teach their children their secrets, and this to me is amazing.

I have so enjoyed and really cherished their gifts. Their strengths and weaknesses have helped me make decisions within my life because they are happy and learned to love and grow as it was hard, and when times became rough, they learned how to wade through these challenges and became stronger and more humble.

God built up character in each and transformed others into completely unrecognizable women by time; he had molded and shaped them in their lives just as he has with me and continues.

I watch my daughters, both so different from the other and so courageous and full of their own unique strengths, and it is amazing that God granted me such a privilege to raise them, be in their presence, and see them grow and face their own challenges.

The truth is God answered my prayers and gave them the insight to be more confident in their young ages that I gush and dwell in thanksgiving for them. I was in my forties before I formally began to actually grow out of one my shells that I was accustomed to, little by little.

Yet it was these women, whom God divinely had put in my path to help guide and mentor me, that made the difference. And I say a forever thank-you to them for God's kindness.

CHAPTER SEVEN

MIRACLES

In every day, we are granted a miracle just on the basis alone that we survived conception to be here.

Knowing that you are literally one out of a million that defeated the odds to unite in the womb and then be birthed out of the womb is grounds enough to believe that there must be a divine higher being.

I was born in a small-town hospital. I was the first delivery to the doctor who helped deliver me.

My mother had to be cut quite extensively to birth me as the choice was given to my father to make the choice—would my mother or the baby live? My father chose my mother, which only stands to reason.

However, my mother fought this decision, and well, as you see, I may have come here being fought for, but I made it.

And as everyone else here before and after me has been fought for, we all have something in common.

We all were born into the bodies we live in, we breathe air, and we all will die eventually, leaving this body behind.

In my youth, I had an accident happen where I lost my ability to talk; I made noises and no one understood me—that is, except my mother.

My parents afforded me a tutor; I was blessed here because monies were tight for them at this time.

I learned how to pronounce my sounds and talk again, and although I had to repeat my first year in school, it was a blessing to be able to talk and be understood.

I remember very clearly the looks on some faces as I would try to sound out words and speak full sentences with no one being able to make out what I was trying to say.

I remember also some people who would rather not bother with a child or take a moment to understand me.

This was difficult, yes! And yet this was God's plan for my life, as he knew I had to face challenges in my life so I could face them and conquer them later.

I was being prepared to face many challenges as I reflect on my life and look back now.

God will take any situation and turn it into a blessing if we allow him.

I have read books and seen movies and heard remarkable stories of war veterans who, while in foreign territories, have beat the odds. Some have missing body parts; others have handicaps we are not able to see yet are able to share their testimonies of valor and courage. Amazingly, most come back with a stronger connection to Christ because they know without a speckle of doubt now who the Father, the Son, and the Holy Ghost are!

So let's blow it wide open!

The Holy Spirit! Some churches are afraid to discuss this, let alone read a scripture about it in the pulpit to their congregation, yet this is who the Father and the Son are as well!

The Bible is full of the Holy Spirit, and in fact, without it, we would not have understanding.

The Son, Jesus, promises the spirit of truth in John 14:15-17:

> If you love me you will keep my command And I will give you another Counselor to be with you forever—the Spirit of truth.

> The world cannot accept him, because it neither sees him nor knows him. But you know him, for he lives with you and will be in you.

Wow, forever! Imagine being able to use this gift as Jesus taught and discern truth! That is a powerful gift!

And keep reading. There's more in John 14:18-20:

> I will not leave you as orphans; I will come to you. Before long, the world will not see me anymore but you will see me. Because I live, you will also live. *On that day you will realize that I am in my Father and you are in me and I am in you.*

Let's break this down. Jesus said, "I am in my Father! And you are in *me*! And I am in *you*!"

This means *we* are all together!

Once you have received Jesus as your Lord and Savior, you are not alone!

Paul again shares during the division in the church about wisdom from the Spirit.

He really wants to drive home a powerful message between God's wisdom and man's, as we can read in 1 Corinthians 2:5-11:

> So that your faith might not rest on men's wisdom, but on God's power. We do however speak a message of wisdom among the mature, not the wisdom of this age or of the rulers of this age, who are coming to nothing.

No we speak of God's secret wisdom, a wisdom that has been hidden and that God destined for our glory before time began. None of the rulers of this age understood it, for if they had they would not have crucified the Lord of glory. However it is written,

No eye has seen,

No ear has heard,

No mind has conceived

What God has prepared for those who love him,

But *God has revealed it to us by his Spirit.*

The Spirit searches all things, even the deep things of God. For who among men knows the thoughts of a man except the man's spirit within him? In the same way *no one knows the thoughts of God except the Spirit of God.*

All right! This is exciting because now we can be certain we do not have to rest on man's wisdom! We also know that this is a message spoken among the mature!

And this wisdom is God's secret wisdom.

God destined for our glory before time began.

Clearly, God had preplanned ahead before time began! This is what God reveals to us by his Spirit! This is an amazing find!

We have already recently learned from the book of John when Jesus shared the following:

"I am in my Father!

And you are in *me*!

And I am in *you*!"

God shows up!

It says in Ephesians 1:13-14, "And you were included in Christ when you heard the word of truth, the gospel of your salvation. Having believed, you were marked in him with a seal, the promised Holy Spirit."

God has marked us with a seal!

We have the promised Holy Spirit!

According to Revelations 1: 8, "I am the Alpha and the Omega. Says the Lord God. Who is and who was and who is to come, the Almighty."

We are alive in Christ!

Is there anything here that is selfish?

Absolutely not!

God gave us everything, equipped us to defeat, win, and conquer!

There are different kinds of gifts and

The following is stated in 1 Corinthians 12:3-11:

> Wherefore I give you to understand, that no man speaking by the Spirit of God calleth Jesus accursed: and that no man can say that Jesus is the Lord, but by the Holy Ghost.
>
> Now there are diversities of gifts, but the same Spirit.
>
> And there are *differences of administrations,* but the *same Lord.*
>
> And there are diversities of operations, but it is the *same God* which worketh all in all.
>
> But the *manifestation of the Spirit* is given to every man to profit withal.
>
> For to one is given by the *Spirit the word of wisdom*; to another the *word of knowledge by the same Spirit*;
>
> To *another faith by the same Spirit*; to another the *gifts of healing by the same Spirit*;

To another *the working of miracles*; to another *prophecy*; to another *discerning of spirits*; to another *divers kinds of tongues*; to another the *interpretation of tongues*:

But all these *worketh that one and the selfsame Spirit,* dividing to every man severally as he will.

CHAPTER EIGHT

TRUTH

The truth is we can do all things through Christ who strengthens us.

I desired to really share the Holy Spirit because too many Christian are afraid to.

The truth is you can't teach the word of God without the Spirit, as Jesus is of the Spirit and God the Spirit, hence the Father, the Son, and the Holy Spirit.

Got it? Good.

Have you or anyone you may know ever had that feeling about something you should perhaps do or perhaps not do? That's God! That's the nudge. If we're in tune with our lives, we will feel, see, or hear. That's the Holy Spirit when he relates to me.

Now to share some things, 99 percent of Christian leaderships won't do. I know this is probably going to raise some voices, hairs, or at the very least stir some thoughts out there among you.

To start with, I'm just going to throw it here.

I'm not perfect. Nope, I'm not!

I have done things that a Christian should think about before doing.

And as soon as I've done them, I knew that conviction, a nudge, or the Holy Spirit let me know right away.

A while back, as I was driving home during rush hour traffic, a car cut me off.

I had to brake forcefully for that car to fit in front of me (we will refer to the person driving as *her* or *she*). She forced her vehicle in front of me!

This happened so quickly that I could feel the red heat up in my face.

And the awe of this is that every day, and on most other days this has happened, I was fine with this type of traffic behavior.

I first raised my hand and held it up to my head so the other driver could see in her rearview mirror, and I did a handshake-type or wave motion next to my head, signaling to the other driver that I thought she was *crazy*!

Well, at this point, we were now communicating with signs because, of course, she flipped me off with her middle finger, so I blew out a kiss gesture. The type of kiss I blew was not intended at this moment to be at all well intended but sarcastically given.

She moved eventually to the other lane, and then the traffic light turned green, and she got through the light and I didn't.

Hmmm. I was given a moment to reevaluate my behavior on this.

Well, this is how a relationship with Christ works. Let me explain better what I mean. As I was reflecting now at the light signal, I saw into myself and was disappointed.

In having a relationship with Jesus, you will desire to work on your behavior and self to become more like him. I felt disappointed in myself for allowing a traffic incident to negatively affect me. The positive is I now have a built-in willingness button to desire to change toward better behaviors. My relationship with Christ is like when you would make friends with someone new. Each of you assesses the other and fit in.

I knew I behaved badly as I sat in my vehicle at the light; I had time to think about this and asked God for forgiveness because I may not see that driver again.

And sincerely I haven't yet; if I'd had the opportunity to see her, I would've said "I'm sorry." You see, I'm not perfect. Yet I do have an automatic willingness to change. I've been on automatic now for twenty-seven years.

This began the moment I received Jesus Christ into my heart. He has taken me up!

I was a wreck—a wretched, depressed, dark human—and he has walked me clearly into his desire when I made this decision to allow Jesus into my life, for his will to be done in me, through me, and all around me.

I can honestly say what a patient God we serve.

I don't have as many erupted behaviors anymore as this.

And I do have a tremendous amount of more joy, love, peace, hope, and faith in my life.

And I couldn't conceive the idea of wanting it any other way.

Ask and you will receive.

In the times we live in today, it is important to do just this.

We live in a volatile time, and people are afraid to speak up for what is right.

What is good and moral and loving and purely Christlike.

And yet these are the times we need to be addressing the issues at hand and winning this ground for Christ.

He preordained us.

Schools! Country! Leadership! Public prayer! Life!

I believe God does love everyone, and he wishes not for everyone to miss his everlasting and ever-loving plan.

We shouldn't be falling further away from obtaining this, and yet as a Christian who has a loving relationship with God, it hurts as laws have moved in and created barriers to keep me further away from performing or living the open freedom we know God intended for us.

Ask and you will receive.

Why is it we have so many laws of freedom of expression to protect everyone, yet if I want to pray with a group of people in public, I could be asked to leave when prayer has never ever hurt a single soul?

Ask and you shall receive.

According to Matthew 17:20, "Because you have so little faith. I tell you the truth, if you have faith as small as a mustard seed, you can say to this mountain, Move from here to there and it will move. Nothing will be impossible for you."

Nothing will be impossible for you!

A simple challenge: proclaim a prayer-of-faith day every week for five minutes at 7:00 a.m. or 7:00 p.m. every Wednesday for the next year. You can pray for all these things very simply: schools, countries, leadership, public prayer, life! In Jesus's name, we want them back.

And then spend one minute in silence, meditating to Jesus for his will to be done.

The Holy Spirit will begin to lay it on the hearts of some to move for positive change, others to support them, others to build more prayer groups, and still others to give in ways that will undoubtedly create these needs.

I am a very simple prayer warrior; however, I believe in a very big faith!

Our God, our Father, our Jesus, our Spirit is the source to things that can be done!

Glory to God the highest!

You are entitled to stay where you are or grow to any level of means you desire with God.

God is a God of free choice. He did not send Jesus to condemn.

Not all of us live perfect lives, and yet there is not one single soul out here that God wouldn't love to see become his.

How is it that we have so many people—so many walks of life, behaviors, races, cultures—and yet so much in common?

Only because of the oldest existing supernatural power ever to be and *is*. The great *I am*—our God!

I have seen a lot people go through a lot of hard challenges in their lives—divorce, losing a limb, losing eyesight, drug addiction, alcohol abuse, losing homes, losing income or even a loved one, being held captive or in prison, or being in a coma.

And I have seen or heard the testimonies.

God prevails and will and has and still lifts the heavy burdens for all these.

Some people have been put into positions of prostitution, drug trafficking, gang robberies, and murder or war. And still I have seen and heard testimonies of God's intervention come in and dismantle the evil and wronged and heal the misled and the abused and the sick.

This is our world, this is our time, and this is our God. The word of God is the living, breathing Spirit-ordained Jesus Christ, our Lord.

Where I am now since I have been taken up?

I am in a very assured place where the Lord has reassured me with our relationship by his loving Grace. I have had the pleasure of many, many adventures and shortcomings and successes and tried hard moments in time. I hope to share a lot more of them in time.

God has always prevailed with his true word. He has made me a better person.

He has healed me when I was sick, raised me up when I was knocked down, put the enemy at my feet, and stamped out the works of the evil when it came against me. I am a protected child of the most high.

And like a good father, he wants what's good for his children all the time.

And like a good father, he has had to put the brakes on me few times so I could learn and to be equipped to move forward.

I not only raised two daughters, I also raised three boys. I had no idea how to raise boys, nor did I have at my disposal family who lived nearby to help, mentor, or ask for advice on the fly. With no discredit to my family, I would call them long-distance on the phone at times, yet I had my share of challenges, as they did too. What I know is real through all those years was the constant, watchful eye of Christ. I have had the privilege to have spent many moments with each of my sons in prayer for their needs and their hearts and praying for people they love so much and care about that they would be covered by God's blessings. I truly admire my boys as they have also grown and matured to adults. Not any one of them is like the other, yet they do love and care for the other. And this is due to the ever-loving promise and grace of our God.

I, like some, will at times leap into something and become overwhelmed in how to finish it. Also, I have been known to repeat the same efforts many times without getting the resolved end I intended. And sometimes it isn't until I have finally exhausted myself to no end before I finally completely stop what it is that I'm doing, and then and only then do I hear the voice of the Lord, the Holy Spirit, talking to me. We are meant and engineered to success.

We cannot outdream our Father!

He has preordained us. Hmmm, that keeps coming up.

Just think of a party planner. Someone who takes care of all the details to assure that you will have a most memorable experience. They think of everything for you. The place is planned and then staged, and the guest list is made, the decorations and what will be served and table settings and the place settings that go on the table are picked, maybe a guest book and cameras are set out, parking is arranged, and invitations and maps are sent out. And the event is under way.

The who or who's it took to plan will be rewarded.

All this and in many cases more.

When our Father preordained our lives, he not only made plans for one moment in your life, but for your lifetime.

And he detailed every living day to orchestrate perfectly in timing to the world you are living in. He did this with a love so grand and with such enthusiasm and light and has marked you for all successes.

He knows your heart. And he knows what you are capable of.

He has you in the palm of his hands.

Whether it's my homeless friend on the street or my millionaire friend in his second mansion, our Father loves and our Father cares and Our Father promises.

After all, this is the Creator of the universe; and if he can manufacture the destiny of the moon and stars and sun, every living creature on earth, every mountain, every plateau, every river that flows unto the oceans' ends,

he can and he has made that individual time and, as promised, continues with *you*!

Our Father has asked for your commitment to him to receive his son Jesus as your Lord and Savior.

No money can buy or bargain this. And no big house or amount of gold can be given to him as a bargaining tool for his eternity.

No high-ranking official can threaten him.

This had been tried already over two thousand years ago!

When I received Jesus into my heart, not only did a relationship begin, but an incredible journey also. I always knew I was being looked over. It gave me a confidence I needed to move in and out the corridors of challenges I would meet. Although I wasn't always happy with myself, I did learn.

And I learned with a very patient teacher.

It was warming to know and feel his presence as I still do today. And it still is a wonderful feeling to know that our Father cares and is so sovereign and is today, yesterday, and tomorrow forever here for *us*!

When two or more believers get together and believe, *anything* you ask shall be done! Isn't that great news?

You don't just belong to the "I do believe" club, but you belong to the "It is done" club!

Faith

As I pointed out earlier in the book of Matthew, it is stated that "I tell you the truth, if you have faith as small as a mustard seed, you can say to this mountain, Move from here to there and it will move. Nothing will be impossible for you."

Grasp the idea that nothing is Impossible for *you*!

And yet, here is some instruction given us in Thessalonians 5:16-22 that I find useful:

"Be joyful always; pray continually; give thanks in all circumstances, for this is Gods will for you in Christ Jesus. Do not put out the Spirit's fire; do not treat prophecy with contempt. Test everything. Hold on to the good. Avoid every kind of evil."

Who else could have inspired many books to be written, published under one cover, and withstand the best sellers for over two thousand years and counting? And proclaim all the winning battles of war, feed the multitudes with a couple mere crumbs of bread and a few fish, and heal every sickness and disease? Care enough to build mountains, desserts, and running rivers and every living thing there is? Take a dozen and more criminals and turn them into walking teachers for his name and then sacrifice it all for us at the cross because he loves us so much?

You got it! Jesus Christ.

There comes that moment in life when we all face a time when we really have questions about our belief systems and those around us. The confusing rat race can be wearying at times. There is one sure place you can go to that will always be available and always be looking forward to seeing and being with you.

If you haven't made that decision yet and you feel it is time, please say this simple prayer:

Dear Lord Jesus,

Please come into my heart. Be my Lord. Be my savior. Please forgive me of all my sins.

I receive you, Lord Jesus, and believe I have been forgiven of all my sins.

I am now saved by the Blood of the Lamb in Jesus's name, Amen.

If you have prayed this prayer and made Jesus your Lord and Savior, please confess this to a friend, a loved one, or even a stranger, or you can write me and let me know.

The Promising Word
PO Box 41870
Mesa, AZ 85274

Please tell someone, and please keep your faith growing, and get into a Bible-based, Jesus-believing-centered Church.

I hope you have enjoyed reading, as my target is to share the love and encouragement of Jesus Christ. It has truly been a blessing to share with you.

Please don't be afraid to pass this book along to a friend or buy another one and pass that one on too. I will be in touch again, sharing and encouraging more as the Holy Spirit blesses. With love and God's richest blessings until later, amen.

Edwards Brothers Malloy
Thorofare, NJ USA
June 19, 2012